Nicaragu

Ernesto Cardenal

Nicaraguan New Time

translated by
Dinah Livingstone

illustrations by
Armando Morales

Journeyman

First published in Great Britain 1988
by the Journeyman Press Limited

The Journeyman Press Ltd, 97 Ferme Park Road
Crouch End, London, N8 9SA and
Journeyman/Kampmann & Company Inc, 9 East 40th Street
New York, NY 10016

Journeyman *Chapbook* 16

*paper*1 85172 027 8
*cased*1 85172 028 6

First printing 1988
10 9 8 7 6 5 4 3 2 1

Cover designed by Ingrid Vandergucht

Computer typeset from disc in Garamond 11/13
by Wordstream Ltd, Poole and printed in Great Britain
by Richard Clay Ltd, Bungay, Suffolk

TRANSLATOR'S ACKNOWLEDGEMENTS

I'd like to thank all those who helped me with this book, in particular, in Managua: Julio Valle-Castillo, who gave me a wonderful Nicaraguan dictionary, Enrique Duarte, Humberto Quintanilla, Silvio Linarte and other Nicaraguans who introduced me to their country; Alun Burge of CIIR; naturalists Cindy Taft and Mauricio Araquistain. In London I'd like to thank the poet Kathleen McPhilemy, Gillian Shaw, librarian at the Institute of Latin American Studies, for her help with the American Indian terms, and the library staff at London Zoo and Kew Gardens.

CONTENTS

PRINCIPAL WORKS BY ERNESTO CARDENAL

1952 *Con Walker en Nicaragua*
1959 *La Hora Cero*
1960 *Gethsemani, Kentucky*
1960 *Varios 'no'* translation of *A Few Don'ts* by Ezra Pound
1961 *Epigramas*
1965 *Oración por Marilyn Monroe y otros poemas*
1966 *El Estrecho Dudoso*
1967 *Salmos*
1969 *Homenaje a los Indios Americanos*
1970 *Vida en el Amor* (prose)
1972 *En Cuba* (prose)
1972 *Canto Nacional*
1973 *Oraculo sobre Managua*
1975 *El evangelio en Solentiname* (prose)
1976 *La Santidad de la Revolución* (prose and poetry)
1981 *Tocar el Cielo*
1985 *Vuelos de Victoria*

INTRODUCTION

Ernesto Cardenal was born into an upper class family in Granada on the shore of Lake Nicaragua on 25th January 1925. He studied at the University of Mexico (1943-7) and in graduate school at Columbia University (1947-9), where he came under the influence of Ezra Pound. He returned to Nicaragua in 1950 and became an active member of the revolutionary group UNAP (National Union for Popular Action). In 1952 he was arrested and imprisoned by the National Guard for one of his political epigrams. He took part in the April conspiracy of 1954 against Somoza, which failed. His epitaph for his friend Adolfo Baez Bone, who was killed then, ends with the famous line 'what they did was bury a seed'.

In 1956 the first Somoza was assassinated by the poet Rigoberto Lopez Perez, also the year of Cardenal's religious conversion. He entered the Trappist monastery in Kentucky, where Thomas Merton was novice-master, studied theology in Cuernavaca[1] Benedictine monastery in Mexico and finished his preparation for the priesthood at La Ceja, near Medellín, Colombia.

In 1965, at the age of forty, Cardenal was ordained in Managua. He set up a religious commune in Solentiname, an archipelago on Lake Nicaragua.[2] In 1970 he experienced his 'second conversion' during a three month visit to Cuba. On 13th October 1977, men and women members of the Solentiname community —

---

1. Here he completed his seminal prose work *Love* (English translation by Dinah Livingstone, Search Press, London 1974).

2. Robert Pring-Mill's translation of *Marilyn Monroe and other poems* (London 1975) has an interesting introduction to Cardenal's earlier work (until 1970).

including Donald, Elvis and Felipe Peña — attacked the San Carlos Barracks across the lake. The National Guard retaliated by breaking up Solentiname and Cardenal was forced into exile in Costa Rica. In 1979, after the triumph of the Sandinista Revolution, he was appointed Minister of Culture for Nicaragua. Almost at once he set up poetry workshops all over the country for everyone who wanted to join. Poems from these workshops are published regularly in the Ministry's poetry magazine, *Poesia Libre*.

The poems brought together in *Nicaraguan New Time* — eight before and twenty two since the Revolution — have been selected as an introduction to Cardenal's life work. Before Somoza's overthrow Cardenal was a prophet, both denouncing — at considerable risk to himself — the dictator's evil regime, and creating Nicaragua's new society in his 'heart's imagination'. Shortly after the Triumph, one of the graffiti on a wall in León read 'The Triumph of the Revolution is the Triumph of Poetry'. Cardenal was one of the poets who came to power. Now his prophetic and poetic vision had a chance to be fulfilled; he became an *acknowledged* legislator. Shelley, a poet who remained one of the unacknowledged legislators, urged the people of England to:

> Rise like lions after slumber
> in unvanquishable number.
> Shake your chains to earth like dew
> which in sleep had fallen on you.

Cardenal can say: 'And we did it.'

*　　*　　*

This selection starts with two poems from *Homenaje a los Indios Americanos* (*Homage to the American Indians*: first published in 1969 two years after his *Psalms*). In the first poem, 'Katun 11 Ahau' (*katun* is a Mayan word for a period of time: about twenty years), the *chilan*, the wise priest-seer, denounces the present bad time and foretells a better time to come when there will be 'good rulers for the joy of the people'. Cardenal's role has been like that of the *chilan*, both in the old and the new time.

The other American Indian poem, 'Maizefield', has been chosen for its beauty, and because maize was and is very important in Nicaragua. The Mayans were 'people made of maize', and as a staple Nicaraguan crop and food, in 'tortillas', maize has been used as a constant revolutionary metaphor.

Next come two anti-Somozan psalms. These were published in 1967, one year before the Latin American Conference of Catholic Bishops meeting in Medellín broke their tradition of siding with the conquerors and oppressors, and declared that Christians should make a 'preferential option for the poor' — so providing a charter to liberation theology. Psalms make up most of the Church's liturgical 'office', prayers said at set hours in monasteries. Their transformation here into contemporary political denunciations is a powerful expression of the unity of Cardenal's religious, poetic and political commitment.

After his visit to Cuba in 1970 — his 'second conversion' — the long *Canto Nacional* was published in 1972, dedicated to the FSLN, the Sandinista National Liberation Front. The two short extracts included here foretell better times, like the *chilan*, and like an Old Testament prophet proclaiming what will happen *in that day*: 'In that day the meek shall obtain fresh joy ... and the poor shall exult' (*Is*.29:19). Cardenal, though, prophesies how things will be in more down-to-earth terms, such as 'the gross national product shared among all'. This is because 'first and foremost the Revolution is about loving', and so — as he says in the later poem 'Economic Report' — 'the economic has become poetic'.

Next comes a piece from *Oraculo sobre Managua*, first published in 1973, the year after the Managua earthquake. The title echoes the Oracle concerning Babylon and other Oracles in *Isaiah* 13-23. The brief extract, subtitled 'Leonel Rugama' here, tells why this young Christian poet chose to engage in the armed struggle and join the urban guerillas in Managua. It was because of his vision of a 'City of Communion': 'I know not, oh I know not what *social* joys are there!' as the hymn 'Jerusalem the Golden' puts it. As Managua at the time was a city terrorised by the National Guard, Rugama has the same double vision of the city as Blake, who denounced the current state of things in his poem 'London':

> I wander through the chartered streets
> near where the chartered Thames doth flow ...

and also saw it prophetically as Jerusalem:

> The fields from Islington to Marybone,
> from Primrose Hill to St John's Wood
> were builded over with pillars of gold
> and there Jerusalem's pillars stood ...
> Pancras and Kentish Town repose ...

The City has to be built here on this earth where we are or not at all.

Two poems from the old time have new time pairs. In 'Arrival', Cardenal imagines that when he reaches Managua Airport the Revolution has happened. After the Triumph this dream is fulfilled in 'Another Arrival'. In 'The Peasant Women of Cuá' the women are not just the 'midwives' of change but the mothers, and their cries under torture are the cries of the country in labour; they also have 'subversive dreams'. In the second poem these same women are present and bear witness at a great celebration. Here, as in the prophet Joel quoted by Peter at Pentecost (*Acts* 2), seeing visions and dreaming dreams have proved to be signs of 'the last days', and part of the revolutionary process.

With the poem 'Lights' ('the early morning of the 18th of July. And the beginning ...'), 'Final Offensive' and 'Barricade', when at last it is all happening, we find that this 'new time' is not cyclical like the Mayan *katun*. These three poems have an urgent New Testament sense of time as 'kairos': the 'right time' for something crucial to happen: 'Now is the time of salvation'. 'That day' foretold by the prophets has come. It inaugurates a radically new time, in which something has changed for good. This is making an enormous theological claim, firmly grounded by liberation theology[3] on the gospel (that is, 'good news to the poor'), but it provoked a strong reaction from conservative sectors of the Catholic Church. Ernesto, his brother Fernando, Minister of Education, and Miguel D'Escoto, Foreign Minister, have all been suspended from their priestly duties by the Pope.[4]

The rest of the poems are about the new time. Some are from his book *Vuelos de Victoria* (1985) (*Flights of Victory*), and some have been translated from his typescript — all his unpublished poems to date. The poems tell us about this new time: the joy, the work, the difficulties and the huge cost. In the poem 'Busy' we find

---

3. Of course, this is in no way claiming that Nicaragua is perfect. Liberation theology speaks of 'both now and not yet'. In the sober words of the Rector of the Central American University, Managua: 'The Nicaraguan Revolution is not ... the Kingdom of God, although it has taken justice very seriously as well as . .. other characteristics of common human life, which Jesus in the Gospels and faith in Jesus Christ in the primitive Church designate as signs of God's Kingdom.' César Jerez S.J., 'The Friend who came to drink from the people's well' in *Celebration for Gustavo Gutiérrez* (Orbis, New York 1988).

4. There are interviews with all three in T. Cabastrero, *Ministers of God, Ministers of the People* (Zed Press, London 1984).

Cardenal as a minister in the new government taking part in the realisation of his own prophecies.[5] One of the things to be done 'quickly quickly' is to *change the names* of streets, hospitals, islands, the airport etc. The 'cries of the country in labour' have brought about a saving birth, the Revolution, and now the task for the 'fullness of time' is to *'recapitulate all things in it'*. (The word used in the *Epistle to the Ephesians* 1:10 is *anakephalaioun*.) In contrast, the rather zany poem 'A Minister's Reflections' shows Cardenal pausing from his onerous official duties to contemplate a cat. In 'New Ecology' all creatures groan for liberation, and the Revolution is for them too, just as vice versa, turtles make love in the sea 'for the sake of the human species and its fulfilment, communism.'

In the fifties, Cardenal had begun describing his poetry as 'exteriorist', but some of the poems here have a more personal element. In these he speaks of the hard sacrifice he made as a priest renouncing women and the possibility of his own children. Then he has other very tender poems about children, one about them growing up in the new time, free.

He read the poem 'Free' at the Rubén Darío Poetry Marathon earlier this year. This was a day-long Poetry Marathon, which takes place every January in the amphitheatre in Ciudad Darío Nicaragua and it had just the atmosphere the poem describes of freedom and ease. At the beginning of the proceedings Daniel Ortega spoke for an hour. (In the poem 'Free' Cardenal's mind wanders while a *comandante* is making a speech!) At lunchtime there was free food and rum for all — of which some poets who had already performed in the morning took very good advantage! There was something of the atmosphere of an English country fete, except that,

---

5. There is an interview with Cardenal as poet and minister in Margaret Randall, *Risking a Somersault in the Air: Conversations with Nicaraguan Writers* (San Francisco 1984).

instead of tea there was rum and hot sunshine, and at the table sat Daniel Ortega, the President, Ernesto Cardenal, the Minister of Culture, and other officials from the Ministry, who also happened to be excellent poets. The courtyard was full of poets, Nicaraguan and some visiting from abroad. At the end of a whole day's listening to poetry in the sun, there was a party in the evening, and what should they do to relax but recite more poems! Carlos Rigby, a black poet from the Nicaraguan Atlantic Coast, and powerful exponent of his Caribbean tradition, gave a brilliant performance of a long poem by Rubén Darío, Nicaragua's most famous classical poet. He said that now the people of Nicaragua feel all their past culture belongs to them all.

This same point was explicitly made by Carlos Mejia Godoy, the Nicaraguan poet and musician (also an MP), in a recent concert of his revolutionary songs in the Shaw Theatre in London. Embracing, in his turn, the Atlantic Coast, he included a calypso 'The Coast is a Giant Awakening'. This was followed by a piece in which he took a peasant melody from the North of Nicaragua and a theme from Vivaldi and interwove them into an organic whole, which was beautiful, strong and alive. This is the policy of Ernesto Cardenal's Ministry of Culture. Looking at it from Thatcherite England, we can only feel delighted admiration and wish we could be so civilised.

The Nicaraguan Ministry of Culture sees the Revolution's job as restoring their whole past and present culture to the people — whose wealth it is — just as it is restoring their land. The word *anakephalaioun* in the *Epistle to the Ephesians*, quoted above, literally means 'recapitulate', but has also been translated as 'restore',[6] which is another aspect of the same process. In the Revolution, just as history is recapitulated by *renaming* places and things, culture is restored to its rightful

6. The Latin Vulgate has 'instaurare'; RSV has 'unite'.

owners.[7] And as with the land, those who possess it can both produce and enjoy its bounty.

Nicaragua is a country full of poets, including many in the government, and their importance in shaping the Revolution is enormous. Unlike in England, their political role is taken for granted. In Cardenal's poem 'Meditation in a DC-3' the military pilot shows the map of 'our land below' to a small girl of nine and 'his hand brushed her small hand'. This image conveys very clearly the unique style of the Nicaraguan Revolution — an extraordinary blend of passionate militancy, with a loving sweetness — which makes it perhaps the most human Revolution there has ever been. Tenderness is a word in constant use and a highly valued quality.[8] It is quite extraordinary the feeling in Nicaragua that they really do want to create a loving society — this is regarded as a normal and obvious thing to want to do! — and the extent to which, while facing fearful odds, they are succeeding. Nicaragua's poets, Cardenal in particular, are the creators of this unique revolutionary style, which has made Nicaragua now, in John Cornford's words (a poet who died fighting fascism in Spain, aged twenty like Leonel Rugama): 'heart of the heartless world'.

The poems towards the end of this selection describe some of these fearful odds, the 'Empty Shelves', the

---

7. Unlike in George Orwell's *1984*, this renaming and 'rewriting the history books' is not falsifying; it is merely taking a different point of view. For example, we can agree that William and Mary ascended the British throne in 1688, but we may not want to call it the Glorious Revolution. Some people think Britain's glorious revolution has not happened yet.

8. Cf. the characteristic oxymoron 'armed to the teeth with tenderness'; Tomás Borge's 'Revenge' on his torturers:

> My personal revenge will be to offer
> these hands you once ill-treated
> with all their tenderness intact.

And the song 'Comandante Marcos':

> The enemy firing in his blind fury
> found no force could finish your tenderness.

'Economic Report', 'The Price of Bras' (Cardenal's niece complains). There is 'The Black Folder' on Reagan's desk, and 'The US Congress approves Contra Aid' (rather as in the trial scene in *Alice in Wonderland* the congressmen start turning into animals, but extremely unpleasant ones).

Finally, there are two poems for the 50,000 who died, out of a total population of three million: 'The Parrots' and 'For those Dead our Dead'. At the beginning of the book the poem 'Maizefield' spoke of 'the pyramids of the dead' and 'Katun 11 Ahau' of 'time to build a new pyramid / on the old pyramid'. The last poem in the book, 'For those Dead our Dead', is pyramid-shaped, and ends with the words:

> You represent them.
> They delegated you,
> the ones who died.

Dinah Livingstone
London, May 1988

KATUN 11 AHAU

Katun[1] of many arrows and disgraceful rulers,
sorrow in the huts,
                              whisperings,
                    nightwatches.
In this *katun*
we weep for burnt books
and exiles from the kingdom.
Loss of the maize
and our teachings of the universe.

Greed and plague and rocks and skulls.

Chief Wildcat. Chief Honey Bear.
                              The Jaguar of the People.
In this *katun* the *chilan*[2] writes:
                    'The people eat sticks
                         and stones.'
Katun of collection of tribute,
                    stealing of masks
theft of the treasure buried in the maizefield.
In this *katun* there are always invaders,
enemies of the earth.
Bloodsuckers ...
                    − preying on the people.
Spillers of pots.

How hard is our life in the forest, like *tepescuintles*[3].
They despise our knowledge of the book of the universe
for the protection of the people.
          (In this *katun* they mock at our costumes.)
                    The hieroglyphics are lost in the mountain.
Our civilisation lies under black buzzards.

The hurricane has torn up our houses.
The nobles are labourers digging the road.
The people stoop under their mountain
                    loaded into a net
and governments are like drought ...

And we say: O that he would return
                    who first built an arch,
                        composed prayers,
created the calendar
which made possible chronicles and history
                    and prophecies of the future.
Meanwhile now, we are like *tepescuintles*.

O sad moon,
sad sad moon in the Petén[4] sky.
Oppression ...

                    nightwatches.
The great libidinous Honey Bear.

And the *chilan*, 'he who is mouth', writes:
    'Now there is a great plague and huge hurricane.'
            In the blue sea rises the fin,
                rises the fin
                        of evil Xooc the Shark.

But the *katun* of the Cruel Men will pass.
The *Katun* of the Tree of Life will come
and good government.
And they will not ask the people to eat less,
Katun of Unity with one Cause.
Katun of Good Living.

And we shall no longer speak in hushed voices.
The people will be united, says the *chilan*.
Many will join together in singing.
            Honey Bear will be dead and gone.
The mountain stone will have a beautiful face again.
The stone pillar
            will have a face.

There will be good rulers for the joy of the people.
   Legitimate lords.
Abundance in the mountains and fine ceremonies.
It is time to build a new pyramid
                    on the old pyramid.
Evil Xooc the Shark has been harpooned.

And there will always be *chilans* among the people.
The *chilan*:
              He who reads the sacred scriptures
and studies the night sky,
movements of the sun and moon
to know the time for tilling the earth,
cutting the maize,
              burning the maizefields.
             laying traps
hunting deer in the mountain.

The *chilan*:
He who announces the rain days,
days when people sing,
the end of the rainy season.
He defends from disease and hunger.
He distributes food on hungry days.
He oversees the carving of the stelae[5],
   he designs the new temples,
he delivers the tablets with the eclipses.

MAIZEFIELD

The maize is buried, invisible as the dead
in your maizefield.
       Just earthmounds and earthmounds
like the pyramids of the dead
          in the maizefield of the dead.

But the *chac*[1] will come with their calabashes
      (their machetes flash lightning)
the streaming ones
the transparent *chac*, rain-coloured
who lie in cave waters deep underground
and meet on June nights in the ruins of Coba.[2]

And the *balam*[3] will come, the maizefield guardians
      with their air-coloured bodies
the *balam* who fly over trees invisible
and you hear them whistling, you hear them
at night in the roads whistling off evil spirits.

And the *x-kol* bird will sing in the maizefields
  to make the maize grow:
       grow-there-more, grow-there-more
          (from bush to bush)
       and to make the maize glad.

With the east wind the rains will come,
they will come from the east where the sun rises
      and the moon and stars
from the east where lie the ruins of Coba.

And that is where the dream animals are
      which hunters speak of
long haired creatures speckled or spotted like leopards

strange animals seen only in dreams
who roam the ruins of Coba.

Under the earth the seeds, step by step,
      one step each day
              are climbing the maize pyramid.
The night is full of stars whose brightness
signals rain.

PSALM 5

Hear my words O Lord,
                    listen to my groans
Hear my protest
because you are not a God friendly to dictators
or a supporter of their politics,
you are not influenced by propaganda
and you do not associate with gangsters.

There is no sincerity in their speeches
or in their press releases.

They speak of peace in their speeches
while they increase war production.

They speak of peace in Peace Conferences
and in secret they prepare for war.

                    All night long their lying radios blare.

Their desks are stacked with criminal plans
                    and sinister expedients.
But you will save me from their plans.
They speak with machine gun mouths.
Their gleaming tongues
                    are bayonets.

Strike them O God
                    confound their politics
wreak havoc on their memorandums
                    wreck their programmes.

In the hour of the Alarm Siren you will be with me
you will be my refuge on the day of the Bomb.

Those who do not believe their lying advertisements

or their publicity campaigns
           or their political campaigns
                        you bless
and surround with your love
                as with armoured tanks.

PSALM 57

You defenders of Law and Order
isn't your law on the side of one class?
                  Civil Law to protect private property
                  Penal Law to harass the oppressed
The freedom you speak of is freedom for capital
          your 'free world' is free exploitation
Your law is gunlaw and your order the jungle
          the police are yours
          the judges are yours
There are no big landowners or bankers in prison.

The bourgeoisie go wrong from their mother's womb
they have class prejudices from the day they are born
    as the rattlesnake is born with poisonous glands
        as the tiger-shark is born to eat people.

O God put an end to the status quo
                draw the oligarchs' fangs.
Flush them away like lavatory water
        let them wilt like grass under insecticide.

They are the 'worms'[1] when the Revolution comes
They are not cells in the body but microbes
    aberrations the new human being must blot out.
Before they sow thorns let the tractor uproot them
The people shall enjoy themselves
              in the exclusive clubs
they will take possession of private firms
the just will rejoice in Courts for the People
In great city squares we shall celebrate
    the anniversary of the Revolution
         The God who exists is of the proletariat.

THE PEASANT WOMEN OF CUA

Now I am going to tell you about the cries in Cuá
            women's cries like cries in labour,
Maria Venancia, ninety, deaf and corpselike
            shrieks at the guards: I've seen no lads

and Amanda Aguilar, fifty years old,
            with her daughters Petrona and Erlinda:
                  I've seen no lads
like cries in labour.

Three months in prison in a mountain barracks,
Twenty five year old Angela Garcia
with seven children.
            Candida at sixteen nurses a little girl
                very tiny and ill fed.
Many people heard these cries in Cuá,
            cries of the country in labour.

When she came out of prison
            Estebana García mother of four
gave birth. She had to give her children
         to a farmer. Emelinda Hernandez was sixteen,
            her cheeks shiny with weeping,
her plaits sodden with weeping ...

Captured in Tazua on their way from Waslala
            with the maize in flower
and the taro[1] already tall.
The patrols went in
            and came out with prisoners.

       They took Esteban up in a helicopter
and a bit later came back without him ...

Juan Hernandez was fetched by the patrol
one night and did not come back.
        Another night they took Saturnino
and we never saw him again … Chico Gonzalez
                was taken too.

        This happened nearly every night
        at the hour when the screech owls call
and it happened to others we did not know.
        Matilde miscarried where she sat
when all night long they interrogated her
                about the guerillas.

    A guard called to Candida:
        Come and wash these trousers
        but it was for something else.
(Somoza grinned from a portrait
                like an alka seltzer ad.)
        Others even worse arrived in an army lorry.
Three days after they left
                Candida had her baby.

This is the story of the cries in Cuá
painful as the cry of the screech owl,
the story told by the women of Cuá
        who weep as they tell
seeing through misting tears the prison
        and the helicopter above.
        'We know nothing about them.'

But they *have* seen them
                their dreams are subversive
bearded, blurred in fog
        swift
                passing a stream
hidden in the maize
                pointing
                (like pumas)
                bursting out of the bushes!

bashing the guards
 coming to the farm
(dirty and glorious)

 Candida, Amanda, Emelinda
many a night in dreams of them
 — with their kitbags —
 climbing uphill
 singing with spirit

and Maria Venancia aged ninety
 at night in dreams
 in strange mountains
on many nights
 they see the lads.

From *Canto Nacional*

TO THE FSLN

1

The great peasant co-operatives are coming,
and the literacy crusade is going to begin,
children in Muy Muy will learn ballet,
theatre in Tecolostote, in Telpaneca. Oh vision
of earth with exploitation
done away!
The country's wealth equally shared,
the gross national product shared among all.
Nicaragua with no National Guard.
I see the new day!
An earth without terror. No tyrant dynasty. Sing
grackle[1], sing out your bugle call!

No beggars, no prostitution, no politicians.
Of course there's no freedom while there are rich
at liberty to exploit others,
at liberty to steal.
While classes exist no one is free
We are not born to be slaves
or to be masters.
We are born to be brothers and sisters.

What is capitalism but buying and selling of people?
For what kind of journey is it friends,
where are we going
with First and Third class passengers?
We have nickel awaiting the new human being,
mahogany awaiting the new human being
cattle awaiting the new human being,
now all we need is the new human being.

Come on
comrades let's tear down the wire fences
Break with the past.
Because the past did not belong to us ...
As the Cuban girl told me: 'First and foremost
the Revolution
is about loving.'

2

Now we write this on the walls:

LIFE IS SUBVERSIVE
or
LOVE IS THE AGITATOR

And on the walls with Leonel Rugama we write:

LET YOUR MOTHER SURRENDER![2]

And also on the walls Joaquín Pasos's[3] words:

Go home, go home go home,
go home Yanks go home.

When a *curré* bird sings on a dry tree
it is announcing drought
when it sings on a green tree it will rain.
Get rid of the wire!
Rise up everybody including the dead.

From *Oracle concerning Managua*

LEONEL RUGAMA[1]

It's suicide not to,
you told your friends
in the Cafe La India.
In the middle of the general
                    tendency to disintegration
there is an opposite tendency
                    to union. Love.
Our poor aqueous systems —
solution based on water and salts,
energy in the form of carbohydrates —
                    cry out for, crave
this joining of one with all.
          An opposite tendency that is revolution.

That is why you Leonel Rugama,
twenty year old poet,
                    joined the urban guerilla war.
Ex-seminarian and marxist,
in La India you said revolution
is communion with the species.
          Proclaim that the Kingdom of God is near ...

That is why there in that house
you battled all afternoon.
                    For God is also City:
(God as City:
                    City where each human being
finally meets every other,
                    City of found identity
and fullness of being together,
                    City of Communion.)
For the sake of this City
                    you joined the urban guerilla war.

THE ARRIVAL

We get out of the plane
                    and Nicaraguans and foreigners
all go towards the great lit building — first
Immigration and Customs — and as I approach
passport in hand I think: how proud I am
to carry my socialist country's passport
and what satisfaction to arrive
in socialist Nicaragua — '*Compañero*' ...
they will say to me a comrade revolutionary
welcomed by revolutionary comrades
                    in Immigration and Customs
— not that there will be no control, there has got to be
so that capitalism and Somoza's ways
                              can never return —
and the excitement of coming back to this country
                              in revolution
with more changes every time,
                    more expropriation decrees
they tell me about, ever more radical transformations
many surprises in the short time abroad
and I see joy in all eyes — those who stayed
and those who left — and now we come into the light
and they ask nationals and foreigners
                              for their passports
but it was a dream and I am in Somoza's Nicaragua
and they take my passport with the cold courtesy
with which they would say, 'After you!' in Security
and they take it inside and don't bring it back
(surely they must be phoning — maybe to Security
or the Presidential or who knows where) and now
all the passengers have gone

and I don't know if I'll be detained
but no; they come back with my passport
                            within an hour
the CIA would know that this time I did not go to Cuba
and only spent one day in East Berlin
at last I can go through Customs
I am the only traveller left with my old case
and the boy who checks me behaves as if he is checking
but checks nothing and says to me in a low voice:
                            'Reverend'
and does not search the bottom of my case
                            where he would find
a recording of Allende's last call to the people
from the Moneda interrupted by the sound of bombs,
which I bought in East Berlin, or Fidel's speech
on Allende's overthrow that Sergio gave me
and the boy says to me:
'Eight o'clock and we've not had supper yet,
we Customs officers feel hungry too.'
And I: 'What time do you eat?'
'Not till the last plane's in.'
And now I am making for the dark flattened city
where everything is just the same
and nothing is happening but I saw
his eyes and his eyes said the word: '*Compañero.*'

LIGHTS

Clandestine flight at night.
In danger of being shot down. The night serene.
The sky full, flush with stars. The Milky Way
resplendent through the thick glass window pane,
a luminous pearly blur in blackness
with its millions of processes
of evolutions and revolutions.

We were flying over the sea to avoid Somozan aircraft,
but close to the coast.
The little plane flying low and slow.
First the lights of Rivas,
taken and retaken by the Sandinistas,
now half in Sandinista power.
Then other lights: Granada, in the grip of the Guard
(it will be attacked tonight).
Masaya, all free. So many fell there.
Further off a glare: Managua. Site of many combats.
(The Bunker.) Still a Guard stronghold.
Diriamba, free. Jinotepe fighting. Such heroism
flaming in these lights. Montelimar —
the pilot points it out —
the tyrant's seaside retreat. Beside it Port Somoza.
The Milky Way above,
and the lights of Nicaragua's revolution.
Far away to the North
I think I can see Sandino's bonfire.
('That light is Sandino.')

The stars above us and this earth's littleness
but also its importance and of these
pinpoint lights who are people. I think:

42

everything's light.
The planet comes from the sun. It is light made solid.
This plane's electricity is light. Metal is light. Life's heat
comes from the sun.

'Let there be light.'

There is also darkness.
There are strange reflections, I don't know what from,
on the windows' transparent surface.
A luminous red: the plane's tail lights.
And reflections in the tranquil sea: they must be stars.
     I watch my cigarette's small glow —
it also comes from the sun, a star.

  Shape of a big ship. The US aircraft carrier
patrolling the Pacific coast?
To our right a bright light startles us. An enemy jet?
No. The moon coming out, a half moon, all serene,
                  lit by the sun.
    Danger of flying on such a clear night.

    And suddenly the radio.
Jumbled words flooding the small plane.
The Guard? The pilot says: 'They're our lot.'
             These waves are ours.
And we are near León, liberated territory.
A fiery orange red like hot cigar ash: Corinto,
its bright wharf-lights gleaming in the sea.
And now Poneloya beach
          and the plane coming in to land,
the coast's foam belt brilliant in the moonlight.
  The plane is coming down. Smell of insecticide.
Sergio says to me: 'The smell of Nicaragua.'

    This is the most dangerous time,
above the airport enemy aircraft may be lying in wait
for us. Now the airport lights.
We have landed.
  Out of the darkness loom olive green comrades

and hug us.
We feel their warm bodies,
    which also come from the sun,
which are also light.
            It is against darkness this revolution.
It was the early morning of July the 18th.
            And the beginning
                    of everything that was to come.

FINAL OFFENSIVE

It was like a trip to the moon
with all its precise and complicated details
taking into account all that was foreseen
                    and also what was not.
A trip to the moon in which the slightest mistake
                    could be fatal.
'*Workshop* calling!' — 'Hullo *Assumption*!' —
                    'Hullo *Maizefield*!'
Workshop was León, *Assumption* Masaya,
                    Maizefield Esteli.
And young Dora Maria's placid voice from *Workshop*
saying enemy reinforcements were surrounding them
dangerously,
her calm singing voice:
            '*Workshop* calling! Can you hear me?'
Ruben's voice in Esteli. Joaquín's voice in *Office* —
Office was Managua.
Office would run out of munitions in two days' time
                    ('Over!')
Precise instructions in code where the landing
                    would be ...
And Dora Maria: 'Our rearguard is not well covered.
                    Over!'
Serene calm voices crossing back and forth
                    on the Sandinista radio.
And there was a time when the two forces
                    were balancing,
balancing, and things were very dangerous.
It was like a trip to the moon.
And there was no mistake.

So many working together in the one great project.
The moon was the earth. Our bit of earth.
And we got there.

And now Rugama[1],
it's beginning to belong to the poor; the earth is
(with its moon).

BARRICADE

It was everyone's job.
Those who left without kissing their mother
so that she would not know they were going.
He who kissed his girlfriend for the last time
and she who left her lover's arms to embrace a FAL[1].
He who kissed his granny acting as mother
and said he was coming back, took his cap
            and did not come back.
Those who spent years in the mountains. Years
clandestine in cities
            more dangerous than the mountain.
Those who carried letters along dark northern paths
or drivers in Managua,
            drivers for guerillas every nightfall.
Those who bought arms abroad
            by dealing with gangsters.
Those who trod the carpets
            of a president's audience room.
Those who attacked barracks
            to the cry of 'Free country or Death!'
The boy on watch at the corner of a liberated street
with a black and red handkerchief over his face.
Children humping paving stones[2],
            tearing up paving stones from the streets
                — they were a business of Somoza's —
and heaving paving stones and paving stones
            to make the people's barricades.
Those who brought coffee to the lads on the barricades.
Those who did the important jobs
            and those who did the less important ones.

This was everyone's job.
The truth is we all piled up paving stones
in one big barricade.
It was everyone's job. The people together.
                              And we did it.

ANOTHER ARRIVAL

Just after the triumph, the first week,
we were coming home from Cuba
  the Twenty Sixth of July celebrations.
I was remembering Fidel's speech
and Marti's phrase: 'It's all glory in July.'
And suddenly, blue on blue appears the Monotombo[1],
free for the first time since the Indians.

Tender green square fields, daybreak.
                    Lake Managua rosy in this dawn,
the small Bird Isle near Managua
(it was Somoza's too,
the first Somoza wanted to change its name
  to Love Isle)
and I realise now the land looks *more beautiful*.
I say so to Dora Maria[2] sitting beside me
also gazing entranced at our liberated country
this dream we are all dreaming never to awake.
        This beauty used be sort of uncomfortable ...

How lovely the country's looking now.
  How stunning nature looks without Somoza.
How thrilling over the dawn pink lake
to hear the Cubana Airline hostess's announcement
we are about to land at
                    'Airport Augusto César Sandino'.

The plane was full of guerilla *comandantes*.
Now we can drop without fear
  (and of course we don't need passports)
and we go through Immigration
  and we go through Customs
            and they address you as '*Compañero*'.

52

THE ARRIVAL OF THE WOMEN OF CUA

And the great act of the masses
was also attended by the women of Cuá.
The wife of Jacinto Hernandez who fell at Cuskawas.
Bernadino's wife.
                    Amanda Aguilar.
A Cuá delegation.
                    They also brought children.

They recalled the pain, the 'Cuá Happenings'.
Cuá that would not tell where the guerillas were.
            Amanda Aguilar knew a poem about it.
(Amanda Aguilar was a pseudonym,
    her name is Petrona Hernandez.)
The women were taken with their children
    to the Cuá command post.
                    'Some of us were expecting.'
They lost their homes.

Angelina Diaz said:
    'We were going from one place to another
                        over the mountain.'

And Bernardino's widow:
    'Beaten, filthy and blindfold, they took him away.'
A story that isn't forgotten, said Juana Tinoco.
They told of small children tortured.
        Small children screaming in that command post.
        'It was to make them tell who we gave food to.'

And Bernardino's widow:
'He had a sick child that he was minding in the loft.
    The guard arrived and shouted to him to come down.
            He said: I am tending my nipper.

The lieutenant he said to me:
    Say goodbye to your hubby now
                    you won't see him again.
I went walking along behind him.'

Bernardino Diaz Ocho, the one who said:
                    'We are not birds to live on air
                    we are not fishes to live in the sea,
                    we are humans to live on land'
When they took Bernadino away the maize was green.

And Bernardino's wife also related:
'They twisted his tongue out with a winder.
They banged nails in his ears.
They asked him: How many guerillas pass by?
                    Do you know Tomás Borge?[1]
When they murdered him
            the guards were knocking back liquor.'

    There it was always night-time, night and day.
Until the triumph of the lads' revolution.
Then it was like a hood being pulled off.
Amanda Aguilar brought the guerillas food.
        These things were told by the women of Cuá.

They arrived poorly dressed
with a placard that read: Women of Cuá! Present!
        This was the the newspaper announcement
of the arrival of the peasant women of Cuá's delegation.

BUSY

We are all very busy
the truth is that we are all so busy
in these difficult and joyful days
                which will not come back
                            but which we shall never forget
we are very busy with confiscations
                        so many confiscations
so many land distributions
everyone taking down the street barricades
                    to let cars through
                    barricades in all the districts
and changing street names and district names
                    from their Somozan ones
unburying those who were murdered
repairing bombed hospitals
            – this hospital will be called so and so –
creating the new police
listing artists
taking drinking water to this place or that
and these others want electric light
                    the light the dictator cut off
quickly quickly restore the installations
                water and light for Sandino City
    – they decided to call their district Sandino City –
we are very busy, Carlos[1]
the markets must be clean, they must be tidy
                and we must make more markets
we are creating new parks, and of course new laws
        quickly we ban pornographic advertisements
the price of basic grains is well controlled
it is time to make new posters

quickly quickly we must name new judges
quickly mend the roads
and how lovely! we must also build new roads
local council elections
now is the time for a million people to learn to read
you go to your cabinet meeting, you to your union
vaccination for children all over the country
and education plans right now
mechanical rubbish sweepers
      — Monimbo with marimbas[2] again —
fields buzzing with tractors
already there is an association of farm workers
seeds, insecticides, credit, new awareness
and quickly we must sow the fields quickly
and now is the time for new songs
workers returning with joy to their noisy wheels
brother, all the urban bus routes are running again
      — and so many local cultural festivals
    politico-cultural acts they call them now —
and masses said every day for fallen comrades
and there is a new word in our everyday language
            '*Compañero*'
all this will remain for people to read about
    in old newspapers
in yellowing newspapers the beginnings
    of a new history
         poetic newspapers
they will see in beautiful headlines
    what I am telling you now
about these intoxicating days that won't ever come back
these days when we are so busy
because it's true we are *very* busy.

A MINISTER'S REFLECTIONS

What to do? I am Minister of Culture,
going to a reception at some embassy or other.
Which one? Does it matter?
This one or that, so what?
And suddenly on the lawn by the gutter:
                              a cat.
Our two headlamps engage the cat's two eyes.
I'd like to stop here,
                    take a good look at the cat,
                              see the colour of it
(all colours are the same at night the saying goes)
                    watch what it does next,
how it moves its back.
Staying by the gutter with the cat
                              my cat
would be better
            although that
                              would make me a copycat
of Marianne Moore
— for example that cat of hers with a rat in its mouth
and its tail trailing like a shoelace.
Davenport says of Marianne Moore: 'The poet
is more interested in the ostrich
                    than the ornithologist who wrote
Ostrich in the Encyclopedia Britannica.'
And I go on thinking about the cat and Marianne Moore.
            No more.
Now I have gone into the lit embassy
            and I am greeting the Ambassador.

MIDNIGHT IN MANAGUA

Lying in bed in Managua
I was dropping off
                to sleep and suddenly I wondered:
                        Where are we going? We are
in the earth's dark half,
                the other half is lit.
We'll be light tomorrow
                and the others in darkness.
Here in my bed tonight
I can feel
                the journey.
                        But what's our destination?

Now I recall
                numbers learnt long ago:
Travelling at 30 kilometres a second round the sun
and with the sun through the galaxy at 250 kilometres
                                        a second
                and what about the galaxy
how fast does it travel . . .?

Rest quietly Felipe Peña[1] fallen we don't know where
and Donald and Elvis buried
                        near the Costa Rican frontier.
Rest quietly lads, we are going well.
                Spinning in black space
wherever we are going, we are going well
and going well, as well,
                        so is the Revolution.

NEW ECOLOGY

In September more coyotes were seen
        round San Ubaldo.
More alligators shortly after the triumph,
        in the rivers near San Ubaldo.
            More rabbits in the road and grisons[1] ...

      The bird population has tripled, they say,
        especially the tree duck.
The noisy ducks fly down to swim
        where they see the water shining.

Somoza's men also destroyed
        lakes, rivers and mountains.
    They diverted rivers for their estates.
The Ochomogo dried up last summer.
The Sinecapa dried
        because of the great landowners' tree-felling.

The Matagalpa Rio Grande ran dry during the war,
        over the plains of Sebaco.
They built two dams on the Ochomogo
        and capitalist chemical waste
crashed into the river
        whose fish staggered like drunks.

      The River Boaco has filthy water.
The Moyuá lagoon dried up. A Somoza colonel
stole the lands from the peasants and built a dam.
The Moyuá lagoon for centuries so lovely where it lay.
      (But now the little fishes will come back.)
      They felled and dammed.

      Few iguanas in the sun, few armadillos.

Somoza sold the green Caribbean turtle.
They exported sea turtle and iguana eggs in lorries.
　　　　　The caguama turtle is becoming extinct.

José Somoza has been putting an end
　　　　　to the sawfish in the Great Lake.
Extinction threatens the ocelot
　　　　　with its soft wood-coloured pelt,
and the puma and the tapir in the mountains
　　　　　(like the peasants in the mountains).

And poor River Chiquito! Its disgrace
shames the whole country.
　　　　　Somoza's ways befouling its waters.
The River Chiquito of León, choked with sewage,

and effluent from soap and tanning factories,
white waste from soap, red from tanneries,
its bed bestrewn with plastic junk,
                      chamber pots and rusty iron.
That was Somoza's legacy.
(We must see it running clear and sweet again
                  singing its way to the sea.)

All Managua's filthy water in Lake Managua
and chemical waste.
                  And over in Solentiname,
on the isle of La Zanata a big white heap
              of stinking sawfish bones.

But now the sawfish and the freshwater shark
can breathe again.
Once more Tisma's waters mirror many herons.
It has lots of little grackles,
              garganeys, tree ducks, kiskadees.

    And flowers are flourishing.
Armadillos are very happy with this government.
      We are recovering forests, streams, lagoons.
We are going to decontaminate Lake Managua.

Not only humans longed for liberation.
All ecology groaned. The revolution
is also for animals, rivers, lakes and trees.

THE TURTLES

It was in the Pacific.
     Off the coast of Nicaragua.
We were out fishing for red snappers
in the blue sea with the blue sky
     the sea like blue ink
and suddenly two turtles, coupled
one mounted on the other
     making love in the sea
as they had been doing
     since the beginning of their species
to reproduce their kind
     and produce more species and more species
the same act in the sea for millions of years
for love
of the human species
and its fulfilment
communism.
The act that had gone on since the world began.
And I think of Matthew nineteen verse twelve:
And there are those who do not marry
for the sake of the kingdom of heaven, communism —
like a lonely turtle in the middle of the Pacific
     alone under heaven
        wedded to heaven.

REMEMBERING SUDDENLY

On my last days in the world
when I was about to become a Trappist monk
I met a pretty girl at the seaside
who was going to be a nun.
                    What's more she was my cousin.
I remember those legs.
            Their curves like the curve of the coast.
Her skin was brown as the sand on the beach.
Naked, except for what her swimming costume hid.
                She was going to marry God.
                    A wedding with God!
I thought what good taste God had.

Mother Ana is still a nun
but with the Nicaraguan Revolution in full flood
she is a reactionary one.

ELVIS

Elvis Chavarría,[1] I dreamt you
                     were alive on your isle Fernando
in Solentiname, your mother's isle
you did not fall
after your San Carlos Barracks assault,
and were fetching me to meet your new child
                          like the little one you had had
the dark little girl
                  yours and just like you they said
and I envied you this new baby
              because you could do what I was denied
although it was self-denial
           then I awoke and remembered you are dead
         and your isle Fernando is called
                 Elvis Chavarría now,
       you can no longer have
          that new child to take after you
any more than can I,
      you are dead like me
        although we are both alive.

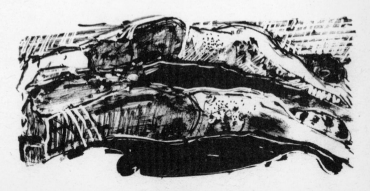

FREE

Comandante, when we
        were with the Association of Sandinista Children
and in your speech you said a phrase
a simple phrase
             'now we are free'
                (together with other phrases)
the very moment you uttered it
I saw children bumbling about the terraces,
some going up, one tiny one laboriously climbing down,
           one eating an ice cream
It was a jumble, a bit of a shambles, the cheerful crowd
        of children and young people
as the voice blared
              through the loud-echoing microphone,
and I felt all these children were free and knew it,
the seven year old sucking his ice, free forever,
they will grow up free,
like the comrade who told me on the way
he thought he would never be able to go by car
                     along a road
when he used to look down from the mountain
                  and see the guard
         and the EEBI[1] men go by,
and he would always have to remain clandestine
                or in the mountain
or like the peasant from El Jocote near Palacaguina,
who said that now he went to festivals
                at night-time unafraid,
unafraid of that helicopter that carried off peasants
        who never came back,
whereas before he had felt like a caged bird.

66

All this flashed upon my sight when you said that phrase
and went on to other phrases, *Comandante*.

MEDITATION IN A DC-3

I don't know why I remembered Novalis' phrase:
'Touching a naked body is touching heaven'.
The military pilot opened his map of our country
        to show the dark little girl of nine
(it was our land below)
and his hand brushed her small hand.
Down there lay Muy Muy, rivers,
        Nueva Guinea where Felipe fell.
                    'It's touching heaven ...'
        But what if they don't believe in heaven?
Of course it's not the high blue sky
        that's earth still
and flying a DC-3 up here
        in our liberated country's atmosphere
is earth.
But the infinite black starry night
with our Earth full of human beings loving one another
        and all the other loving Earths
                    is heaven
                the kingdom of heaven.
So what did Novalis mean?
        For me he is saying:
breastfeeding a baby,
a couple deeply caressing,
holding hands,
clasping a shoulder,
human touching human,
human skin meeting human skin
is putting your finger on communism *compañeros*.

APPARITION IN HAMBURG

A thousand people listening to my poetry
and three hundred in the street who can't get in
    — you know, the publicity,
        your fame ... the Nicaraguan cause —
all the faces in the dark (for me)
    the whole auditorium behind spotlights,
        darkness thundering applause,
but in the light, just near me
almost on stage, and sharing the glare with me
I saw you,
      shorthaired, a bit untidy
eyes the colour of muscatel grapes
   sometimes ocean-coloured out to sea
   or between green and a tender blue perhaps
     (like heaven looking at me)
   that same mouth
     mouth I drank in mine,
girl of eighteen
like that other thirty years ago,
but German, I suppose, this time.
Now I can only look at her secretly
she is with me in my bright space
   in front of the blinding spotlights
on a bench. Then
about three more women comrades, then the dark.
Thus it was that out of a thousand faces
hers was the only one I saw.
For who warned me you would be there again,
you whom He, with a capital H,
              snatched from me
whom I left to embrace the Invisible,

my beautiful ex-seraph I kissed so much but not enough
                    mouth I drank
here again, 30 years on,
                        lips slightly apart
in a smile
eyes suddenly disturbed, desiring
angel,
like that angel yearning
with lust less angelic than bodily
my lovely girl, my street urchin, I kissed
in Las Piedrecitas under the stars, do you remember?
I hugged her in a man's jacket,
mine, lent her for the cold.
I exchanged her for God,
        for God I sold her,
                        was I the loser?
I exchanged you for sorrow.
        Applause for my poems
    with chanting in Spanish
        NO PASARAN
and I can only look at her secretly.
            Pale apple skin
like the apple fresh from the tree
I bit into later that night in my room in the PREM hotel,
sharp, sweet, greenish, juicy, flesh
but it was fruit and nothing else.
        NO PASARAN
it was like losing her again
being given her back and giving her up again.
        A hard renunciation,
            still hard, lifelong,
and now another renouncing
swift this time,
                but still difficult enough, painful,
among clapping in darkness,
the pain of your being her again
and also, perhaps worse, your not being.

71

German girl, I suppose,
            who knows nothing about all this
that the other one knows who was once like you,
      my darling who was eighteen then
         (she knows these lines are for her)
      in that dreadful Somozan night
the lights of the dictator's palace
reflected in Lake Tiscapa.
She who admired my black hair, do you remember?
'Jet black!' you once called it
in that restaurant.
                  The darkness clapping
my poems:
'A love song was their battle hymn
            'If Adelita . . .'
And I meanwhile like our war wounded
crippled
sitting calm in their wheel chairs.
But there was no bomb.
There was an anonymous phone call
   about a bomb the police did not believe.
We would have died together, my love,
I in the news for a day
   fast fading as the blossom on the tabebuia[1] tree
      'when the golden tabebuias were in flower'
            and you
simply a German girl (I suppose)
with any name
who made me once more give up that other
young and fresh this time just like before
and now they are taking a collection
jute bags heavy with coins and notes;
         and there were about
15,000 marks for the people of Nicaragua that night.

THE PRICE OF BRAS

A niece of mine complains about the Revolution
because of the very high price of bras.
I have no experience of having breasts
but I think I could cope with breasts without a bra.
My friend Rafael Cordova
lives near the hamlet of Esquipulas
and he told me many funerals used to pass
along the road
                         with tiny coffins
four, five, six, eight funerals
         every afternoon,
they were children's funerals
                         each afternoon.
Old people did not die so often.
And not long ago the Esquipulas undertaker
came to him:
'Doctor, I need a little help from you,
         I am out of business.
There are no funerals now in Esquipulas.'
In the old days there were cheaper bras.
Now in Esquipulas funerals are far fewer.
You tell me: which is better?

EMPTY SHELVES

Yesterday I went in a supermarket
    and saw the shelves all bare;
most of them empty; and I felt a bit
of the bleakness of that emptiness
    but also I felt delight
for our people's dignity there
    plain to see in that doing without.

These shelves once groaned
with many-coloured unnecessary
and necessary things
or were like in other lands.
It is the price exacted from
    a small country fighting the Colossus,
and I see the empty shelves
loaded with heroism.

    The cost of independence. And because
there are thousands of Sandino's cubs
at large in the mountain.
And just as we no longer
have those rows of coloured goods
neither do we have the lady slumped on the pavement
displaying her open sore
or the marble-white-eyed child with held-out hand.

    The children are playing near their homes;
the grown ups are peaceful
and the police in the streets have no rubber truncheons
to beat people
    or teargas bombs
or waterhoses or riot shields
    because of the empty shelves.

Bare shelves lacking
necessary and unnecessary things
but stacked with sacrifice and pride.
A country's pride, arrogance if you will
the empty shelves.

We will not surrender, we will not sell ourselves.
And I went out feeling sad but glad
because of the empty shelves.

ECONOMIC REPORT

I am surprised to find myself reading
                          with great interest
things like
    cotton harvest twenty five percent up
on last year
                coffee exports US$124.2 million
    17.5% up on last year
a 13.6% increase in sugar is expected
                maize production down -5.9%
    gold 10% down
because of contra attacks in that region
likewise shellfish ...

When did such data ever interest me before?
    It is because now our wealth
                          however little
        is to be
                for everyone.
                      So it is
    for the people,
                love of the people
this interest.
    Love is now the meaning of these figures.

Gold dug from the earth, solid sun
cut into blocks, will become electric light
drinking water
                for the poor. Translucent
molluscs, reminiscent of women, the smell of a woman,
come from the sea, its submarine caves
and coloured gardens of coral to be
pills, desks.

Matter's holiness.
Mother, you know what a glass of milk is worth.
 Soft cloud-whirl cotton
 — we went singing to the cotton-cutting,
 in our fingers we held clouds —
will become, roads, zinc roofs,
the economic has become poetic
 or rather, with the Revolution
economics now is love.

THE BLACK FOLDER

In a windowless basement
in the White House west wing
full of signs saying:
>   Top Secret *Top Secret* TOP SECRET
>   every night is spent by experts
>   starless underground
loading a map of the terraqueous globe
for the twenty four hours just gone
with bits of information from all their sources
>   satellites watching China
>   spies in Poland
>   diplomats in Red Square
contra advisers on the Honduran border
putting it all in a black folder for the president
to find on his desk after breakfast next day
the globe's daily destinies dependent
on what is loaded night after night
in the windowless basement
and placed every night on Reagan's table
in the black folder.

THE US CONGRESS APPROVES CONTRA AID

The senator sings out his speech in his baritone voice
beautifully modulated. Up and down the scale
like playing a trumpet arpeggio with frequent
runs,
      now it's a clarinet,
         the long concatenation of tangled words
            exquisitely articulated in every syllable
      syl-la-bis-ing
neatly the difficult bits of his bad prose
with virtuoso diction.

The next speaker
         in language florid,
           high flown, grandiloquent,
quoting large chunks of James Monroe by heart
as if reciting
      not looking at the script,
raising his voice (and face)
         and suddenly dropping
to a deep bass.
      He sits down sweatily
acknowledging the not very warm applause.

      Bertilda washes her son's wounds,
and says: 'Early this morning I was going to make coffee
and I saw them beating a boy in the street
so I shouted: "Contras!"
      The boys started shooting,
there were just two of them
      and about a hundred contras.'
      The boys were her son and nephew.
'What did I feel? I felt nothing, I just thought:

If they kill them they'll have to kill me.
>I loaded three rounds for my nephew
>because my boy was hurt.
I tied up my two-year-old so she couldn't run about.'

Again:
Heady cocktail of timbre and tone modulations
with anastrophes,
>prosopopoeias here and there,
>>ingenious paronomasias
and sonorous anaphoras.
>His tropes resound in the the decorated chamber
and the decorations echo them back,
few present in the chamber at the time
but his peroration addresses a multitude
>>(hence the applause).

>'Surrender you bastards!' shouted the guard.
'Let your mother surrender!' answered Oscar Leonel
>as if he were the other Leonel come back to life.
The cottage destroyed
by a barrage of grenades and mortars.
The hamlet desolate.
>When the contras left
they scattered Christ propaganda.

'Thirty million in humanitarian aid for the contras.'
>'No sir, thirty eight!'
>>One of the humanitarians titters.
Another bangs the table as if trying to break it
big two-handed swipes like swinging a bat
'There is no graver problem today (*bang*)
and I shudder to speak of it (*bang*)
than the danger (*bang*)
of communism in Central America (*bang*).'

>They killed my uncle,
and his son Ramon, both died fighting.
>Ramon's six year old boy

they murdered in his bed,
he was asleep and they shot him.
He was wounded and asked to see his dead father.
He stroked his face and said:
    'Look, they've made a hole here.'
        And just then the child died too.

Thirty eight million humanitarian aid for the contras.
Night-coloured trousers, jacket and shirt,
    sharp incisors
        bloodsucking lips
          Vampyrum spectrum
  He emits from his mouth and nostrils
similes, prolepses, apostrophes,
      tuneful alliterations,
repetitions, entreaties, preteritions, digressions,
snorts from his warty snout
antithesis, synopsis, synonyms, antonyms.
And resumes his seat. Like a bat hanging upside down.

    Twisted zinc, burnt planks and poles.
What would have been the co-operative.
Still smoking two days later.
On the hill
    the catholic chapel on fire.
      And the little school. The health centre.
  Antibiotics in ashes.
    And buzzards wheeling, wheeling.
Juan Antonio aged fifteen
      fought beside nineteen-year-old Estreberto.
A bullet in his chest
and he crumpled on to Estreberto's knees.
About thirty contras got Mario
and slowly, slowly cut his throat,
    the blood flowed on to the Christ propaganda.

    The Texan senator strikes a dramatic pose
      right foot forward,

arms akimbo like a bronze statue,
they bring him a glass of mineral water.
                        Still in dramatic pose,
                left foot forward this time,
        he is reading the speech they wrote for him.

In the burnt out chapel where the altar was,
Estreberto stops: 'Hell! my dad's blood is still here.'
Tearless eyes. They just grow smaller.
Estreberto saw about twenty attack Leonardo.
They stabbed him.
Juana said she saw only the fireballs.
She looked for Enriquito, aged three,
                and found him asleep.
                        He was dead.
How could she carry him
                weighed down with the others?
        'Not through those god-forsaken brambles.'
She left him in the mountain, near a spring.
She covered him with a parrots' plantain leaf
                        for a shroud.

With a quiver in his voice
to indicate strong feelings under control
slowly, not reading, reciting his speech:
'There are convincing proofs (*pause*)
of the conspiracy of international communism (*pause*)
to export revolution (*pause*)
from Nicaragua (*pause*)
to our borders (*pause*)
and one of the ... (*pause*) to help the contras (*pause*).
Arms trembling as if playing the piano.
        The usher brings him iced water.
A claw is raised requesting to speak.
    Order motion.
The Honourable ...
        With just a little parrots' plantain leaf
I had to leave him there.

They hear the guards laughing.
Lucia so lovely with a bullet in her face.
Lidia they raped and carried off.
The coffee beans, cottages, animals, everything.
   'The children's blood soaked my dress.'

THE PARROTS

My friend Michel is an army officer
   in Somoto up near the Honduran border,
and he told me he had found some contraband parrots
waiting to be smuggled to the United States
   to learn to speak English there.

There were 186 parrots
          with 47 already dead in their cages.
He drove them back where they'd been taken from
and as the lorry approached a place known as The Plains
near the mountains which were these parrots' home
   (behind those plains the mountains stand up huge)
the parrots got excited, started beating their wings
     and shoving against their cage-sides.

When the cages were let open
   they all shot out like an arrow shower
        straight for their mountains.

The Revolution did the same for us I think:
It freed us from the cages
     where they trapped us to talk English,
it gave us back the country
     from which we were uprooted,
their green mountains restored to the parrots
     by parrot-green comrades.

    But there were 47 that died.

FOR THOSE DEAD OUR DEAD

When you get the nomination, the prize, the promotion,
think of the ones who died.
When you are at the reception, delegation, commission,
think of the ones who died.
When you have won the election and the crowd
congratulates you,
think of the ones who died.
When they clap as you go up on the platform
with the leaders
think of the ones who died.
When they come to meet you at a great city airport,
think of the ones who died.
When it's your turn to take the microphone,
be on television,
think of the ones who died.
When you are the one giving out certificates,
passes, permits,
think of the ones who died.
When the little old lady comes to you with her problem,
her bit of garden,
think of the ones who died.

See them stripped, dragged,
pouring blood, hooded, smashed,
kept underwater in troughs,
electric shocked, eyes gouged out,
throats cut, riddled with bullets,
flung to the roadside
in holes they dug, common graves,
or simply lying on bare earth
as future wildflower food:

You represent them.
They delegated you,
the ones who died.

NOTES

'Katun 11 Ahau'

1. *Katun*: recurring Mayan period of 7200 days (just under twenty years). The Spaniards arrived in the first year of one particular Katun 11 Ahau (i.e. 1541).

2. *Chilan*: Mayan priest-prophet, wise man.

3. *Tepescuintl*: from the Aztec *tepetl*: hill, and *izcuintl*: dog. Cloven-hoofed rodent a bit bigger than a rabbit, like a small tail-less pig. The usual Nicaraguan name for this animal is *guardatinaja* ('pot-guard'). Although the general meaning is 'it's a dog's life', Ernesto Cardenal told the translator 'it is a noble animal'.

4. Petén: a region covering the north of Guatemala and the southern part of the Yucatan peninsula where the Mayan civilisation flourished.

5. Stelae: upright slabs bearing sculptured designs or inscriptions.

'Maizefield'

1. Coba: ruined Mayan city, now an archaelogical site.

2. *Chac*: Mayan rain gods. The principal Mayan rain god was called Chac Mool.

3. *Balam*: Mayan deities. Some of the *balam* had second names such as Balam Akab, Balam Quitze. The Mayan pantheon was complex and stratified with numerous deities and supernatural beings.

'Psalm 57'

1. 'Worms' ('gusanos'): the name given to Cubans who did not support the Revolution in their country and fled to places like Miami.

'The Peasant Women of Cuá'

1. Taro: tropical food plant grown mainly for its starchy roots.

'Canto Nacional'

1. Grackle (*Quiscalus macrourus*): common Nicaraguan bird. The male is a brilliant metallic blue black and is also known as a 'clarinero' ('bugler') because its song sounds like a bugle call.

2. 'Let your mother surrender': Leonel Rugama's reply when called upon by the Guard to surrender (see note to 'Oracle concerning Managua'). The Canadian writer Margaret Randall suggests a good translation would be 'Up yours!'

3. Joaquín Pasos (1914-47): Nicaraguan poet, member of 'Vanguardia' group. There is a selection of his poems in Joaquín Pasos, *Poemas de un joven*, selected and introduced by Ernesto Cardenal (3rd edition, Managua 1986).

'Oracle concerning Managua'

1. After leaving the seminary, Leonel Rugama joined the urban guerillas in Managua. He died on 15th January 1970 when the National Guard surrounded him and two others in their safe house near the Cementerio Oriental — with lorries, tanks and helicopters. When the Guard called upon them to surrender, Leonel replied with the (very Latin) super-insult expressing total defiance: 'Let your mother surrender!' His mother and aunt now keep a bookshop in Esteli, and told the translator he did what he did 'because he had such a good education'. His poems are collected in *La Tierra es un satelite de la Luna* (4th edition, Managua 1985).

'Final Offensive'

1. Leonel Rugama wrote a famous poem called 'The Earth is a Satellite of the Moon' about the cost of the Apollo space flight.

'Barricade'

1. FAL: a type of rifle.

2. The paving stones used to make the barricades are chunky octagonal blocks, about 1 foot (about 30cm) at their widest. Somoza embezzled the 1972 earthquake relief money to make himself a profitable business out of them.

'Another Arrival'

1. The Monotombo: a volcano.

2. Dora Maria Tellez: '*Comandante* 2' in the assault on the National Palace on 22nd August 1978. At present she is Minister of Health (also see poem 'Final Offensive').

'The Arrival of the Women of Cuá'

1. Tomás Borge: One of the ten founders of the FSLN (Sandinista National Liberation Front) and the only one still alive. He is now Minister of the Interior.

'Busy'

1. Carlos: Carlos Fonseca, one of the founders of the FSLN, and revered leader of the Revolution. Killed in the forest of Zinica, 8th November 1976.

2. Marimba: a musical instrument like a giant wooden xylophone with hanging resonance pipes.

'Midnight in Managua'

1. Donald Guevara, Elvis Chavarría and Felipe Peña: members of the Solentiname community who took part in the assault on San Carlos Barracks on 13th October 1977. Donald and Elvis were caught shortly afterwards by the Guard and murdered. Felipe was captured in the assault, imprisoned, and liberated with sixty other political prisoners after the FSLN took the National Palace on 22nd August 1978. He then joined the Front in Nueva Guinea (a region in the south of Nicaragua) and died not long before the Triumph of 19th July 1979.

'New Ecology'

1. Grison (Latin *galictis* – several kinds): a weasel- like animal common in Nicaragua.

'Elvis'

1. Elvis Chavarría: a member of the Solentiname community, captured and murdered after the attack on San Carlos Barracks on 13th October 1977. Some of his poems appear in *Poesia Campesina de Solentiname*, edited by Mayra Jiminez (Managua 1980).

'Free'

1. EEBI: Basic Infantry Training School. Ferocious National Guard

elite troops under the command of Anastasio (Tacho) Somoza Porto-carrero, known as 'El Chiguin' ('The Kid'), the last dictator's son.

'Apparition in Hamburg'

1. Tabebuia (*tabebuia crysantha* – Nicaraguan: 'cortes'): a common Nicaraguan tree with bright yellow, sweet- smelling, short-lived blossom.